The Story of
NIM
The Chimp Who
Learned Language

by

ANNA MICHEL

Introduction by

HERBERT S. TERRACE

Photographs by
Susan Kuklin and Herbert S. Terrace

Alfred A. Knopf · New York

For Frances Foster and Robert Michel

With special thanks to all of Nim's teachers and friends who appear with him in this book: Jean Baruch, Joyce Butler, Penny Franklin, Maggie Jakobson, Stephanie LaFarge, Jennie Lee, Joshua Lee, Lisa Padden, Laura Petitto, Susan Quinby, Dick Sanders, Jerry Tate, and Bill Tynan.

Grateful acknowledgment is made to the following for permission to use their photographs: The Baltimore Sunpapers, pages 11 (bottom left), 14; Bailey H. Kuklin, page 59; Stephanie LaFarge, page 4; Laura Petitto, page 38; G. A. Tate, pages 32 (bottom right), 33, 57.

This is a Borzoi Book published by Alfred A. Knopf, Inc.

Text Copyright © 1980 by Anna Michel
Introduction Copyright © 1980 by Herbert S. Terrace. Photographs Copyright © 1979, 1980 by Herbert S. Terrace.

Library of Congress Cataloging in Publication Data
Michel, Anna. The Story of Nim: the chimp who learned language.
SUMMARY: Relates the story of Nim, a chimpanzee who is being taught to use sign language to "talk" as part of a program to study language acquisition by animals. 1. Chimpanzees—Psychology—Juvenile literature. 2. Human-animal communication—Juvenile literature. 3. Mammals—Psychology—Juvenile literature. 4. Sign language—Juvenile literature. 1. Chimpanzee—Habits and behavior. 2. Human-animal communication. 3. Sign language. I. Terrace, Herbert S., [date] II. Kuklin, Susan. III. Title. QL737.P96M54   599'.884   79-17501
ISBN 0-394-84444-0   ISBN 0-394-94444-5 lib. bdg.

Manufactured in the United States of America   10   9   8   7   6   5   4   3   2   1

Introduction

Imagine a chimpanzee running through the halls of Columbia University. A young woman is frantically chasing after him. The chimpanzee looks around and hoots with excitement as he runs faster. Then he goes through an open door into a classroom full of people. Leaping onto a desk, he runs around the room, hopping from desk to desk, hooting and grinning all the time. Finally the chimpanzee is cornered. The young woman starts making motions with her hands. The chimpanzee watches her; then he makes motions, too. They are carrying on a conversation in American Sign Language.

TEACHER: *Nim! You bad!*
NIM: *Nim sorry.*
TEACHER: *You very bad.*
NIM: *Me sorry. Hug me.*
TEACHER: *Come here.*
NIM: *Hug me. Hug me.*

This book tells the story of the excitement, adventure and hard work that lies behind this simple but fascinating conversation between Nim and his teacher.

Many people believe that language is unique to human beings and that the ability to communicate through language is the most important difference between humans and non-humans. But in recent years there have been research projects that have shown that apes can also learn words as long as they do not have to speak them. A chimpanzee named Washoe and a gorilla named Koko were each taught signs of American Sign Language. Another chimpanzee named Sarah learned to use plastic chips of different shapes and colors to request various foods, to name colors and to describe actions and spatial relationships such as *in* and *out*, *on* and *under*. With the help of a computer, a similar language called "Yerkish" was taught to a chimpanzee named Lana.

As a psychologist I was intrigued by these experiments. I found the evidence that apes could learn words convincing, but I was skeptical that they could combine these words to create sentences. In order to satisfy my curiosity about this basic feature of all human languages, I began to think about starting my own research project to teach an infant chimpanzee to use American Sign Language, the language formed by hand movements and facial expressions that is used by hundreds of thousands of deaf people.

Dr. William Lemmon, Director of the Institute for Primate Studies, had agreed to let me have the next chimpanzee that was born there, if I would return it to them when my project ended. When he called to tell me a chimp had been born, I jumped at the opportunity to adopt it, and Project Nim was launched. The chimp was named Nim Chimpsky in honor of the famous linguist, Noam Chomsky, who has argued that only humans can master the creative aspects of language.

We know that children learn best when they are happy, well-loved and cared for. Thus it seemed clear that if Nim were to learn to use language in human ways, he should be given the kind of love and care that a human infant experiences. In as many ways as possible, Nim's upbringing was similar to that of a human infant's.

For the first eighteen months of his life, Nim lived with a family in a house in New York City. When he needed more room, Columbia University made available a much larger house in Riverdale, New York, where he was looked after by four teacher-caretakers. At the tender age of ten months he began to go to nursery school five days a week in a specially designed classroom at Columbia.

Nim's teachers not only had the job of being substitute parents and reliable baby-sitters, they also had to know sign language and how to record everything Nim signed. In addition, they had to be able to capture and hold Nim's attention by thinking up interesting activities through which sign language could be taught.

The records kept by Nim's teachers provided me with the most complete information ever collected on the use of sign language by a chimpanzee. From December 15, 1975, to February 14, 1977, we recorded more than 20,000 of Nim's combinations of two or more signs. Even though he was not taught words in sequences, and he was not required to sign more than one sign at a time, Nim combined words to create simple sentences.

To all of us who worked and communicated with Nim, it seemed obvious that he was creating his own sentences in much the same way that a human baby would. But I still didn't have the conclusive evidence to prove scientifically that Nim's sequences of signs were actual sentences. Proving something *scientifically* means ruling out as many other explanations as one can think of. To show that Nim was creating sentences, I could not simply point to interesting examples in which Nim seemed to use language like a human. I had to show that these examples were not just happy accidents. That is, I would have to demonstrate that a vast majority of his combinations obeyed grammatical rules. I would also have to show that he wasn't merely imitating the grammatical combinations his teachers made. It would take more time to gather this kind of evidence — and money.

A research project such as Project Nim requires vast resources. A complete school system was devoted to Nim's education. A large house and companions were required for his daily needs. We also needed computers, videotape equipment, a photo lab, and a large and well-trained staff to run the project. As the needs of the project grew, it became more and more difficult to raise money for it.

Ultimately, as new sources of funds became increasingly scarce, I had no choice but to fulfill my promise and return Nim to his birthplace. There he would spend the rest of his life in the company of other chimpanzees. After four wonderful years, Nim's part in the project came to an end.

Anna Michel, the author of this book, was typical of the many volunteers who worked on Project Nim — a remarkable group of people who became caught up in the exciting idea of engaging a chimpanzee in conversations in sign language. In order to be an effective teacher, Anna had to learn sign language, how to teach it to Nim, and how to keep careful records. Like all of Nim's teachers, Anna also had to commit herself to a rigid schedule in order to keep Nim's day-to-day life as consistent as possible.

Here, from the point of view of one of Nim's steady companions, is the story of the joys and frustrations of trying to teach Nim to communicate in sign language.

HERBERT S. TERRACE
Columbia University
New York, N.Y.

November, 1979

The Story of Nim

On NOVEMBER 21, 1973,
at the Institute for Primate Studies in Oklahoma,
a baby chimpanzee was born.
Though he was just like any other newborn chimp,
he would someday be very special.
He would become one of the first chimps
who could "talk" to people.

*N*ews of the birth soon reached Dr. Herbert Terrace, a scientist at Columbia University who was doing research in the field of behavioral psychology. He was interested in how language is learned, and he wanted to find out if animals could use language as people do. Herb knew that animals could not make the many sounds people make when they speak, so he hoped to teach a chimpanzee to "talk" with its hands — the way deaf people do. The director at the Institute for Primate Studies, where chimpanzees are raised for scientific research, wanted to help Herb with his work. And so, two weeks later, the baby chimpanzee arrived in New York City, where he would take part in an amazing experiment in animal communication. The little chimp was named Nim Chimpsky, and the experiment would be called Project Nim.

Dr. Herbert S. Terrace and Nim Chimpsky

Nim's first family

Herb Terrace thought that if Nim was going to learn language and talk about the things people talk about, he should be raised like a human child. So Nim was going to live with a family where he would be cared for and played with, talked to and loved. He would wear clothes, sit in a highchair, and be toilet trained. These would all be things for him to talk about.

Herb arranged for Nim to live in the home of one of his Columbia students, Stephanie LaFarge. The LaFarge household was big and lively. It included Stephanie and her children, fifteen-year-old Heather, fourteen-year-old Jennie, and eleven-year-old Josh; Stephanie's husband, WER LaFarge and often his children; a friend of the family, Marika; and a German shepherd named Trudge. They would all play a part in bringing up Nim, as would the many teachers and volunteers who joined the project to help care for Nim and teach him sign language.

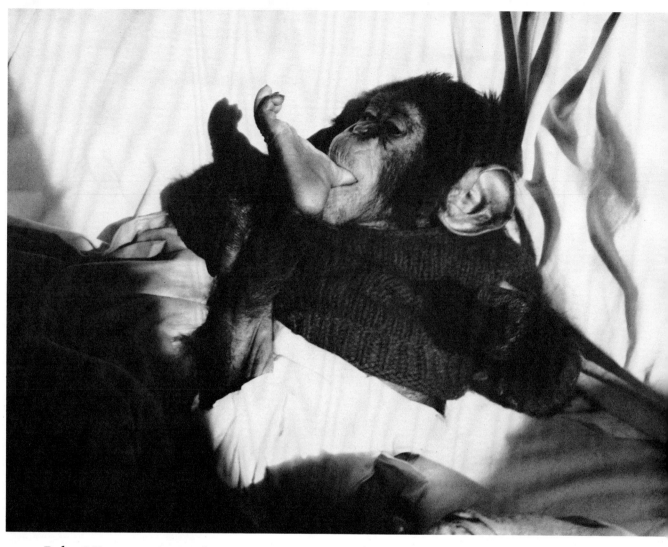

Baby Nim — contented ...

Taking care of baby Nim was very much like taking care of a human baby. He slept in a crib at the foot of his "parents'" bed. Every few hours, day and night, he woke up and cried until someone gave him his bottle. He was fed and burped and diapered. He was held and rocked, tickled and tossed into the air. He smiled and cooed, he kicked and cried, he sucked his thumb — or his toe — and behaved more or less like a healthy human baby.

alert...

Nim became very attached to all the members of his family — especially to Stephanie and Jennie, who took care of him most often during his infancy.

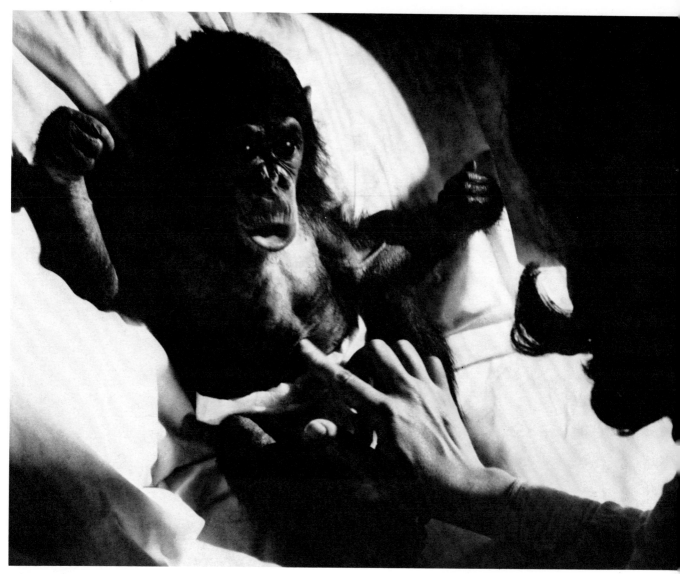

and responsive

From his first day with the LaFarges, Nim was "talked" to in American Sign Language, the language of the deaf. And slowly, in the way a baby begins to understand words, Nim began to understand *signs*. Every time Stephanie brought Nim his bottle, she touched her thumb to her lips making the sign for *drink*. Nim's response was to grunt hungrily and look for his bottle. And when she made the sign *up*, he would reach out his arms for her to pick him up.

Though Nim was beginning to recognize the signs that were being said to him, he made no effort to imitate the signs with his own hands. He had to be shown how to do this. When Nim was two months old, Herb and Stephanie and his other teachers began to gently shape — or *mold* —his hands into different signs. Before Stephanie, or anyone else,

A favorite doll is something to sign about

gave Nim his bottle, she first signed *drink* and then molded Nim's hands to make the *drink* sign. If he wanted to be picked up, she molded his hands to sign *up*. When he reached for a toy, she molded *give*.

Throughout the project Nim's teachers molded his hands whenever they were teaching him a new sign. Eventually Nim even offered his hands to be shaped when he wanted to be shown the sign for something.

"Molding"—a step in teaching Nim to sign

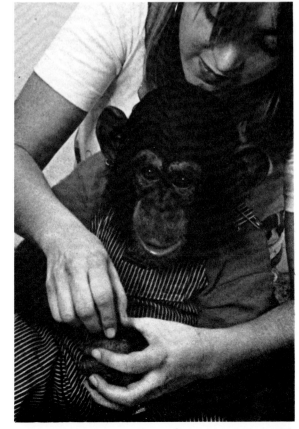

Nim signs *drink*, his first word

One day, when Nim was two-and-a-half months old, Stephanie held up his bottle, and Nim put his thumb to his lips and signed *drink*. This was the first time Nim had made a sign all by himself. Stephanie was very surprised, for no one had expected Nim to begin signing at such an early age. In the next six weeks Nim's vocabulary grew, and he made the signs for *up, sweet, give,* and *more.*

Nim was growing fast and becoming more active every day. By his second month he could both crawl and walk, climb and jump. One of his favorite games was chasing Trudge, the family dog, all over the house. And he always loved a good tickling session or pillow fight with Josh or Jennie. Soon Nim was much too lively to stay in his crib. So a little tent was made out of netting and set up in a corner of the dining room. A hammock was hung inside for Nim to sleep in. At first Nim screamed when he was left alone for the night but then quieted down and fell asleep with a bottle or pacifier.

Playtime...

with "sister" Jenny

Nim's first summer was spent at the seashore. As long as he could keep one of his human friends in sight, Nim ran around happily out-of-doors. He touched, smelled, and sometimes ate the flowers. He tried to catch birds flying in the sky and wild rabbits as they dashed across the grass — always without success. Like all chimpanzees he was afraid of the water, so no one could tempt him into the swimming pool or the ocean, but he liked to play in the sand with his pail and shovel. Efforts to teach Nim were relaxed during this vacation time, and the only new sign he learned that summer was *eat*.

Nim's first summer

When Nim returned to New York City in September, he was ten months old and he knew how to make six signs: *drink, sweet, give, more, up,* and *eat*. Herb decided it was now time to begin a more intensive teaching program —Nim would go to school. There would be fewer distractions in school than at home, so Nim could concentrate more on learning to sign. And it would be easier for Herb to supervise the project if for part of the day Nim was close to Herb's office at Columbia University.

Stephanie and Nim signing *eat*

Nim's school was a group of rooms in the psychology department at Columbia. There was a tiny classroom which would be kept bare so that Nim would not be easily distracted. Next to the classroom there was an observation room with a one-way mirror and a built-in camera. People could watch and photograph Nim from the observation room without Nim seeing them. There was also a storage room for the toys and materials that Nim and his teachers would use; a small gym equipped with a sandbox, climbing rope, and chinning bar; and a diaper-changing area.

When Nim started school his teachers decided it was as important for him to understand sign language as it was to learn to make the signs himself. So throughout the day his teachers signed the names of things around him and talked in sign language about what Nim was doing.

Nim and his "brother" Josh on the chinning-bar

Nim's seventh word: *hug*

On a typical day, Nim would arrive at his school by eleven o'clock. *Hang up your coat*, Nim's teacher signed as she helped Nim take off his coat and hang it on his own hook, just three feet from the floor. Then he usually needed his diaper changed. *Up*, his teacher signed as she lifted Nim onto the changing table. She told Nim to lie down, and he was usually cooperative because his teacher was firm. She always let Nim know exactly what was expected of him. When she removed his diaper, she made the sign *dirty* before dropping it into a garbage pail. Then she reached for the baby powder and Nim became suddenly attentive. This was the part of diapering he liked. As the powder was sprinkled on him, Nim held out his hand to catch some and eat it. *Don't eat powder!* his teacher signed. As she got Nim dressed again she identified each piece of clothing in sign language: *diaper, pants, shirt*. Then she signed *hug* before she hugged Nim and carried him into the classroom.

Nim signs *banana*

Time to eat, she would sign next.

Eat, eat, Nim repeated enthusiastically, making the *eat* sign with his own hand. And he made food grunts that sounded like "uh-uh-uh." Then Nim signed *up*, and climbed up into his highchair. His teacher tied on his bib, identifying it in sign language, and as Nim ate, she showed him the sign for each food. Mealtimes were Nim's favorite parts of the day.

Getting Nim to behave as if he were a well-disciplined human child was hard work. If he jumped around too much during a meal, his bowl was taken from him and he was told firmly to sit down. If he dropped his spoon and ate with his hands, the spoon was put right back into his hand. By the time a meal was finished, there was sure to be food all over Nim's face, hands, and highchair. Before Nim was allowed to leave his chair, he was expected to help clean up. His teacher handed him a sponge and signed *clean*, pointing to the highchair. Since Nim was still a baby, a little help on his part was all that was expected, and his teacher finished the job for him.

To interest Nim in his lessons, his teacher often had to make them seem as much like playing as possible. Every morning Nim's toy bag would be brought out. As the teacher peered into the bag of toys, Nim sat down on her knee, bouncing energetically. There was always something new in the bag — a ball, flashlight, tennis shoe, puppet, mirror — so Nim never knew what to expect. Everything that was pulled out of the bag then became the object of a lesson. It would be named and played with and talked about until Nim grew tired of it.

Nim signs *shoe*, eagerly

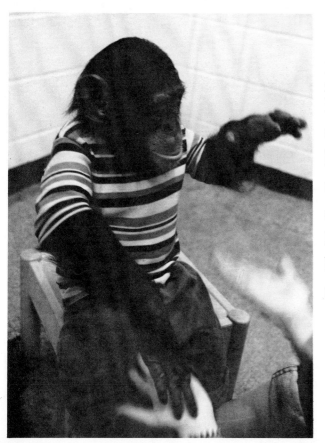

Nim's attention span was short, so his teacher was always ready to move on to a new activity if he became bored or restless. When he was finally tired of the bag of toys, it was put away and a new activity was started. It might be time to look at picture books or work with picture cards, or to draw or paint.

Nim learns the sign for *orange*

Drawing and looking at pictures is part of learning, too

The best way to teach Nim was to tie signing to activities he liked. For example, Nim enjoyed taking a tea break every day, and this provided an opportunity to learn the sign for *tea* and to use some of the signs he already knew. Nim's teacher would use the new sign in many different ways: *Time to make tea; You want tea? I drink tea*, and so on.

Nim makes a cup of tea...and the *tea* sign, bottom right

Learning to make the *tea* sign

When it seemed that Nim understood the meaning of the *tea* sign, the teacher would then mold his hands so he could make it himself. For days or even weeks, Nim only made a new sign right after he had seen a teacher make it. Or he would make the sign at the wrong time, when he really meant something else. Or he would make the sign incorrectly, like baby talk. But eventually Nim reached the stage where he made the sign correctly in the right situation without any help. After three different teachers had reported seeing Nim do this and it had occurred on five days in a row, Herb was confident that Nim really knew the sign. Then it was added to the list of signs Nim had learned.

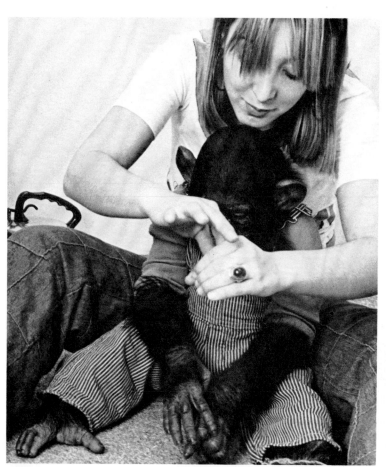

Top: Nim tries to make the *tea* sign   Bottom: He asks for the cup by signing *give*

Next he signs *drink* ...

then *more drink* ...

As Nim got older he not only became more active but also more adventurous. He had to be watched closely all the time — and kept on a leash when he was outside — so that he didn't get into trouble or get hurt.

When a new person joined the project he or she was "tested" by Nim — and Nim could be a handful. He had his own bag of tricks to draw from — behavior that he knew was strictly forbidden — and he could be especially naughty at home. If not kept under control, he would jump on furniture, hang from exposed pipes and chandeliers, climb on the bookcases, and slide down banisters. The more the new person failed to control Nim, the worse his behavior became. He would scratch, bite and hit, and he would break things. How successfully a new teacher stood up to Nim was a test of whether or not that person could work in the project. Nim responded best to friendly but firm handling. He was quick to take advantage of someone who was afraid of him or not strict enough.

At the end of a school day, a good tickling session with Herb

Nim's second home — a twenty-minute ride from his classroom

The LaFarges had grown very attached to Nim — he was almost like one of the family — but by the time he was eighteen months old, it became clear that their home was not designed for a growing chimpanzee. Nim needed much more space. So Herb made the decision to find a new home for him. He wanted a place that could be made "chimp-proof" — where pipes would be covered, chandeliers would be taken down, and Nim would have a room to play in — and where there would be space enough for some of the people from the project to live, too.

Herb learned about a large house that had been given to Columbia University. It had many rooms, and outside there was grass to play on, trees to climb, and even a pond with fish and ducks. It wasn't being used at the time, so Herb rented it for Project Nim. Here Nim would live with four of his teachers. They would become his new family.

Moving day, August 10, 1975, began like an ordinary day. But after school Nim did not return home to the LaFarges. Instead, one of his teachers drove him to the new house. She parked her car outside the fence and pointed to the house, telling Nim that this was where he was going to live. Nim may not have understood, but he was certainly aware of his teacher's excitement. His hair stood on end, and he clung to her. Despite his fears, Nim was curious about the house. As the two of them slowly walked up the driveway, he clung to his teacher's leg with one hand and signed *hurry* with the other hand — a sign he had learned the month before. But once they reached the front door, Nim stopped and refused to walk any farther. *Hug*, he demanded, suddenly wanting the reassurance of his teacher's arms. So she hugged Nim and carried him inside.

Teacher signs *hug*, then *in*

Nim signs *there!*

Nim on his loft bed

As his teacher showed Nim his rooms, she identified each in sign language: *kitchen, gym, playroom, bathroom, bedroom.*

Bedtime was the hardest part of Nim's adjustment to his new home. He refused to sleep in his specially-built loft bed, which had been furnished with a blanket, pillow, and one of Nim's favorite dolls. Instead he spent the first night cuddled between two of his teachers on the floor beneath his loft. It wasn't until the third night in the new house that Nim would even sit on the loft, and then only if someone climbed up with him. A week later, he finally slept alone, but for a whole month he screamed and banged on the door when it was closed for the night.

There was much to see and do and talk about in the new house, and Nim spent those first days exploring and discovering—switching lights on and off, turning on the water faucets, going up and down stairs, opening all the doors, and playing outside. Though at first everything was new and different and confusing, within a few weeks Nim was acting as if he had always lived there.

Investigating the new house

Nim and his teacher sign *house*

Now that Nim's teachers lived with him, more time could be given to talking in sign language, and every daily routine provided something to talk about.

Every morning when it was time to get up, one of Nim's teachers would open the door to his room and greet him in sign language. *Good morning, Nim*. Nim was usually awake but still sleepy, and he didn't answer. As soon as he was ready, he would climb down from his sleeping loft. Then he would take his teacher's hand and lead her down the hall to the bathroom signing, *dirty, dirty*, which was what he had been taught to say when he had to use the toilet. When he was through, he would sign *finish*.

When Nim's teacher held up his toothbrush, Nim signed *toothbrush* eagerly. Brushing his teeth was a task Nim never minded because he loved the taste of toothpaste.

And Nim was always ready to include his teacher in his morning grooming activities.

Nim's morning routine

Next came hand washing. First Nim washed his hands and then, as he got more involved, he washed his feet and even his teacher's hands. When he was finished, he asked for hand cream.

When Nim was younger, the skin on his hands became dry and cracked so applying hand cream had become a daily activity and something else to sign about. Actually the deaf have no standard sign for *hand cream*, but Nim's teachers noticed that when Nim wanted some he always rubbed his hands together. They decided that would be a good sign for *hand cream*. Nim invented one other sign, *play*. In this case, the real sign for *play* was too hard for Nim to make, but when he began to clap his hands in play situations, they decided clapping would be Nim's sign for *play*.

Nim's sign for *hand cream*

Nim signs *shirt* before getting dressed

After Nim had rubbed plenty of hand cream on his hands and feet, and on his teacher's hands too, it was time to get dressed. Nim was expected to name everything he wore before putting it on. Then he dressed himself— sometimes it was easier than others. When he was dressed he asked for a hug and was carried down to the kitchen for breakfast.

Nim's weekday breakfast was usually cereal and fruit. Sunday breakfasts were special — banana pancakes, and Nim helped make them. Since moving into his new home, Nim liked nothing better than being allowed to help with the household work such as cooking, sweeping, and doing the laundry. He watched whatever was being cooked with great interest, and he was allowed to taste it. But tasting didn't seem as important to Nim as having a chance to participate—to help stir, mix, and pour.

After breakfast Nim liked to wash the dishes. *Give*, he signed to get a sponge. Then he would turn on the water, squirt dishwashing soap onto a dish, and rub the dish vigorously with the sponge. This routine would continue for twenty minutes or more until the dishes were all thoroughly cleaned. Then Nim would put them back into the sink and start all over again.

Nim enjoying breakfast ...   cooking ...

eating ...

and cleaning up

Helping with the housework

Nim so enjoyed housework that he often misbehaved when he wasn't included. Once when one of his teachers was in a hurry and didn't want to be slowed down by Nim, she told him he must sit and watch while she prepared the meal. Nim hated being left out and threw himself on the floor, screaming. His teacher didn't pay any attention to him. Since having a tantrum didn't work, Nim tried another tactic. He waited until his teacher looked at him, then he deliberately knocked over the garbage can. Nim certainly succeeded in getting attention this time.

You're bad! his teacher signed. *I'm angry with you!*

Nim hooted and pouted, signing, *Me sorry! Hug! Hug!*

No! You're bad! I don't love you! Nim's teacher wanted him to know that she was really angry. She knew that Nim had learned that by pouting and signing *sorry* he was often forgiven too quickly and his behavior would be just as bad afterwards. She wanted to be sure Nim meant what he was saying.

Sorry, sorry, repeated Nim, becoming more and more upset. He kept running up to her making the *hug* sign, but she would walk away from him. Finally, he scurried over to the garbage can, picked up all the spilled garbage, and put it back into the can. His teacher was still not satisfied. She signed *clean*, and pointed at the sponge. Nim grabbed it and wiped up the floor. By this time all was forgiven.

A hug, and all is forgiven

When the chores were finished, if it was a weekday it was time to get in the car and leave for school. Nim was expected to sit quietly in the front seat and not jump around or reach for anything, and he usually followed the rules. He was curious about everything they passed along the way, especially policemen on horseback or people on motorcycles. He sometimes named what he saw. *Water*, he signed as they went over a bridge; *light*, when they came to a traffic light; and *out*, when the car came to a stop at Columbia University.

Nim signs *come*

On weekends, Nim and his teachers often spent the whole day outside, signing as they worked and played together.

Nim's teachers used small tape recorders whenever they worked with Nim. Each time Nim used a sign, his teacher whispered the word into the tape recorder. Then after a session was over, a report was written. The teacher would listen to the tape and write down all of Nim's signs, along with descriptions of how each was used. The teacher's report also described Nim's behavior and the activities and highlights of the session.

Some of Nim's school sessions were also recorded on videotape. This was an especially good way of recording his conversations when he began to make long combinations of signs — sometimes as many as eighteen connected signs. After a session was videotaped, the teacher would watch the tape in slow motion and write down the entire signed conversation. The tape then became part of the record of Project Nim. All of these records were important to Herb for analyzing Nim's language.

Nim signs *cat*

At the end of each week, a staff meeting was held to discuss Nim's progress. At these meetings, his teachers talked about any problems they might be having with Nim, and they shared ideas about ways to work with him. They also decided what new signs to teach Nim in the weeks to come.

When things were going well, Nim learned one or two new signs every week — but only after his teachers had spent day after day repeating that sign. Old signs were reviewed constantly so that Nim didn't forget what he had already learned.

By the time Nim was three years old, he could make eighty-eight signs. He knew the names of everything he wore, his favorite foods and activities, and the names of many other animals.

He knew his own name and the names of some of his teachers. He was putting signs together to make combinations, such as *me hat* or *give hat* if he wanted the hat his teacher was holding. Or he might sign *tickle me* and *tickle me more*. And like a young child, Nim could understand much more than he could say.

Me hat signs Nim. *Mine!* signs Herb

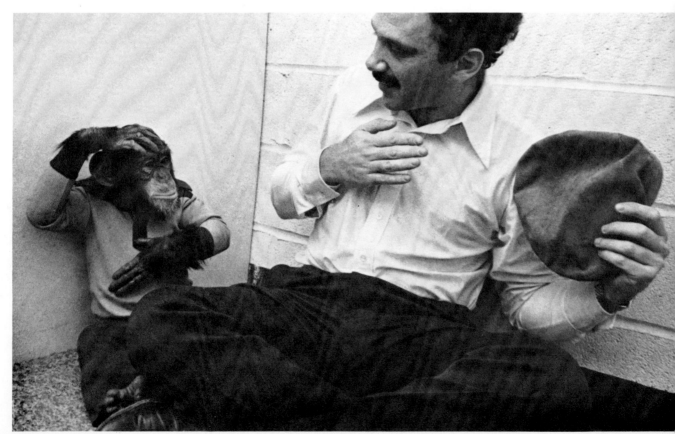

Left: Nim tries to sign *Herb*, but makes a one-handed *cat* sign instead

Right: Herb prompts Nim — two fingers, not one — and Nim struggles to get it right

Below: Success! Nim signs *Herb* correctly with two fingers, the letter *H* in sign language, suggesting Herb's mustache

What? asks teacher. *Eye* signs Nim

Left: Nim requests
a pair of glasses
by signing *glasses*

Nim signs *nose*. Teacher signs *good!*

Nim and his teacher "talk" about *teeth* ... and *ears*

up

down

Some of Nim's other signs

tree

thirsty

gum

42

more

me

play

ball

Nim

Working with Nim demanded skill and ingenuity, and his teachers were always thinking of new ways to make his lessons interesting. One day a teacher brought her cat to class in a carrying case. Nim was curious about everything new, and he was especially excited about other animals. He peeked through the window of the case, trying to find out what was inside. When he couldn't open it, he signed, *open, open, open!*

His teacher was in no hurry. *What's in the case?* she asked.

Open me, Nim open! was his response.

There's a cat in the box, she signed to Nim.

As soon as Nim knew what was in the box, he signed faster. — *Cat, cat hug, cat me,* — anything to get his teacher to open the case

Left: Nim signing *open...*

and *cat...*

When she finally lifted the **cat** out, Nim squealed with delight.

Nim signing *hug* ...

and *cat* again

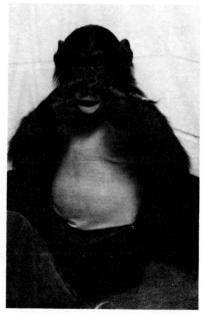

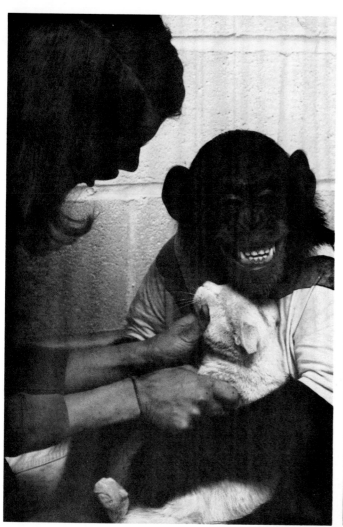

She let Nim hug the cat, and Nim grinned broadly. The cat didn't seem to mind, but the teacher had to keep reminding Nim to be gentle.

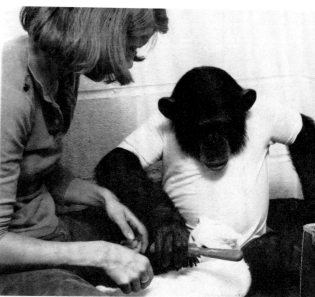

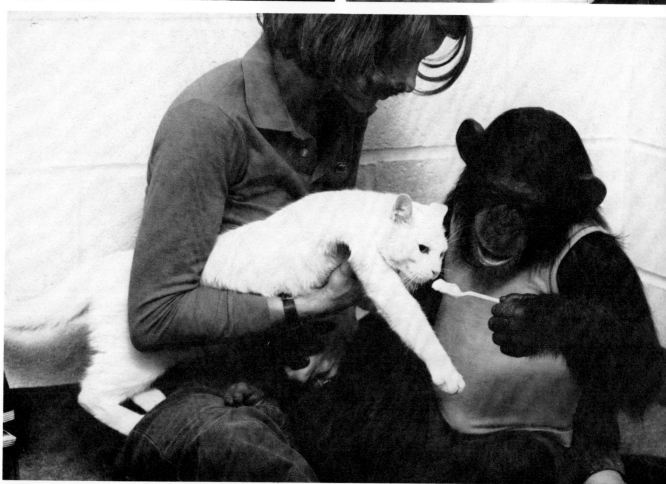

When Nim's teacher held the cat, Nim got jealous. He did whatever he could to get her attention. He jumped onto the cat carrier and hooted. Then he climbed inside.

At the end of the visit Nim kissed the cat goodbye.

Nim learned that he could use language not only to name things and get what he needed, but also to get his own way. His teachers stopped what they were doing whenever Nim made the *dirty* sign, and would take him to the bathroom. So sometimes when Nim wanted to get out of a lesson he had grown tired of, he would sign *dirty* —even though he didn't really have to go to the toilet.

Nim signing *sleep...*   and *dirty*

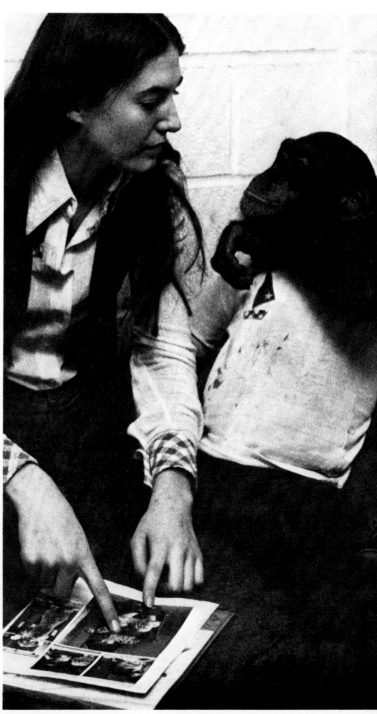

Sometimes he signed *sleep,* even though he wasn't tired. But his teachers learned to tell that Nim was fibbing if he didn't look them in the eye when he made those signs. Sometimes he tried to distract his teachers in the middle of a lesson by starting a game of peek-a-boo or tickling, or by standing on his head. Other times he just didn't pay attention. He looked bored and stared into space.

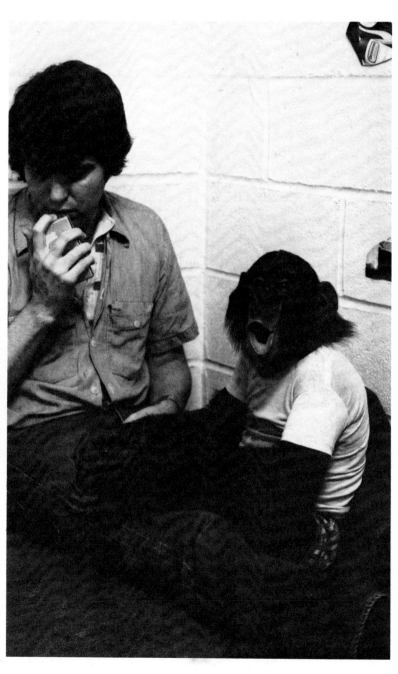

Nim takes some breaks

Use sign language! Herb signs, and Nim begins to sign *tickle me*

When Nim wanted to play instead of work, his teachers had to be firm. *No, it's work time now. Later you will play*, they signed. And they always kept their word. After Nim had worked for an hour or two, they took a break, either in his gym or outside where he could jump, climb, and run around all he wanted. But even during his recess, Nim found things to sign about. He might decide he wanted his teacher to catch him. *Jump*, Nim would sign before jumping into his teacher's arms. And almost every playtime included a request for *tickle* and *more tickle*.

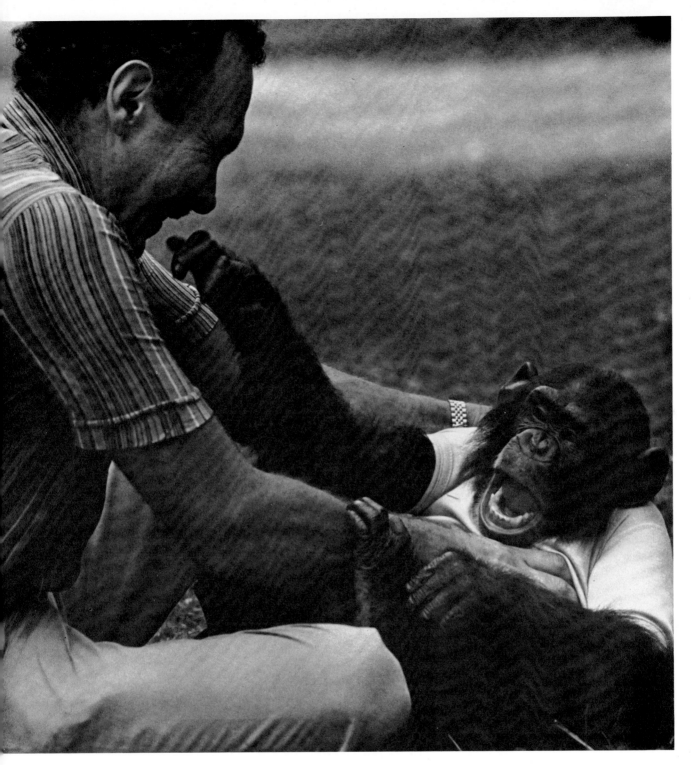

Nim's turn to be tickled

Tickle who? his teacher would ask him.

Tickle me, signed the chimp. Nim laughed in low grunts as he was tickled. And then with a playful expression, he would sign, *tickle you,* and tickle his teacher back. To please Nim, his teachers always laughed hard when he tickled them. Back and forth the game would go.

Playing with Nim could leave his teachers exhausted, but Nim was always ready for more. *Play me* and *play me Nim* were his most frequently repeated two- and three-sign combinations.

Though so much of Nim's behavior was childlike, he also behaved in ways that were pure chimpanzee. He hooted and grunted and walked on his knuckles. He climbed trees and swung from branches.

A chimp at play...

He groomed himself and groomed his teachers. And he made play nests out of twigs and branches the way chimpanzees in the wild do. He did all these things without being taught or without seeing other chimpanzees do them.

and at work ... grooming and nest-building

Herb and Nim

On September 24, 1977, three years and ten months after Nim's arrival in New York City, his part in Project Nim was finished, and he was returned to the Institute for Primate Studies in Oklahoma. There he lives on an island with other chimpanzees who know sign language, too.

Herb has visited Nim since then, and even though over a year had passed, Nim greeted him with hoots of joy and signs for *hug* and *kiss* and *tickle* — not only demonstrating that he remembered Herb but that communicating through sign language was still second nature to him. That pleased Herb, but more important he also saw that Nim was happily adjusted to his new life among chimpanzees.

Long after Nim's departure, Project Nim continued as Herb and his students analyzed masses of data. By the time Nim was retired, he had a vocabulary of 125 different signs. Project Nim had proved that a chimpanzee could not only be taught words in sign language but could learn how to use language to communicate with human beings.

In spite of Nim's accomplishments, Herb Terrace is certain there is still more to be learned from studying the language ability of chimpanzees. If Herb is right, with enough sign language a chimpanzee might someday tell us much — about his past and his future, his feelings and his dreams. Who knows what a chimpanzee might say if he learned the words?

Nim and his new friend, Mack, in Oklahoma

Nim's Vocabulary

(listed in order of learning)

drink	red	flower	berry	cup
up	play	Laura	fruit	bowl
sweet	me	kiss	help	Steve
give	banana	cracker	bad	ice
more	gum	light	baby	run
eat	hat	jump	wash	climb
hug	apple	rock	yogurt	Mary
clean	groom	work	sleep	box
dog	Nim	Andrea	pull	ear
down	key	bite	blue	eye
open	sorry	chair	black	nose
water	orange	pole	paper	shirt
listen	tea	dirty	Joyce	teeth
go	nut	spoon	Bill	throw
tickle	raisin	happy	house	fish
hand cream	smell	Walter	Susan	wagon
brush	pants	angry	thirsty	glasses
ball	you	finish	tree	goodbye
book	bug	hungry	Dick	music
shoe	hot	Herb	lie down	walk
hurt	in	cat	cut	green
toothbrush	powder	pear	napkin	pool
hurry	out	brown	balloon	Bob
come	that/there	bird	cookie	hello
harmonica	please	grape	Renee	peach

58

From left to right:
Anna Michel, Herb Terrace,
Nim Chimpsky, and Susan Kuklin

Anna Michel was a volunteer teacher with Project Nim. She was graduated from Indiana University, received her M.A. from Bank Street College, and studied sign language at the New York Society for the Deaf. She has been a teacher in both nursery and elementary schools and is the author of three nature books published by Pantheon for beginning readers: *Little Wild Chimpanzee, Little Wild Elephant,* and *Little Wild Lion Cub.*

Susan Kuklin is a freelance photographer. She received her B.A. and M.A. from New York University, was a teacher, developed educational materials for the New York City public schools, and taught film studies at the University of Tennessee. Her photographs have appeared in numerous national magazines, and in *Nim* by Herbert Terrace.

Herbert S. Terrace is Professor of Psychology at Columbia University and the founder of Project Nim. He received his B.A. and M.A. from Cornell University and his Ph.D. from Harvard. He has written a book for adults — *Nim* — giving the complete record of the project, is a co-author of two psychology text books, contributor to a number of scientific journals, and a past president of the Society for the Experimental Analysis of Behavior.